I Am Blessed
Meditating on the Scriptures

By Linda Patarello

Unless otherwise indicated, all Scripture quotations are taken from the *KJV Reference Bible*. Copyright © 2000 by Zondervan. Used by permission.

I Am Blessed
ISBN: 978-0-9896919-3-2

Copyright © 2013 by Linda Patarello

Editor: Daphne Parsekian

Published by Orion Productions, LLC.
P.O. Box 51194
Colorado Springs, CO 80949
Orionproductions.tv

These small books with scriptures that fit each theme are meant to help you learn how to meditate. Each scripture has my own meditative thoughts that follow. This will help you understand the thought flow that can happen when you think on God's Word. As you begin to think and ponder on God's word for yourself, you will find more revelation in the Scriptures. The Holy Spirit will reveal it to you personally. I encourage you to read my initial book. How to Meditate on the Living Word. That will explain in more detail the process of meditation.

For now, I will simply state some scriptures that explain the importance of meditating and renewing your mind on the Holy Scriptures—two from the Old Testament and one from the New Testament.

The word "blessed" shows up 205 times in the Old Testament as along with the word "blessing," which shows up 60 times. We have been taught that God is out to strike us and bring us down. This is a lie. When we look up the word "cursed," we see it only 64 times in the Old Testament and "cursing" only 10 times. This should be an eye opener to us.

"And God blessed them, saying, Be fruitful, and multiply, and fill the waters in the seas, and let fowl multiply in the earth."

Genesis 1:22

The first thing that God did was bless. It's as if He said, "Now you go and be a blessing." To be fruitful is to be a blessing; to multiply is all about abundance. So we are talking about an abundance of blessings. Everything that God created was meant to be fruitful and to multiply, from Adam and Eve and their kind on to all the animals, the fish, and their kind. The earth was not meant to be sparse but full and flourishing, rich and lush. This is God's way.

"And he blessed him, and said, Blessed be Abram of the most high God, possessor of heaven and earth:"

Genesis 14:19

Abram was blessed, and not by just anyone, but by the most high God, possessor of heaven and earth. It is God who owns the earth and the heavens. He made and created it and everything in it. They belong to Him. When you think about it, we also belong to Him. It is man which strayed away, not God. In man's rebellion, many think they own their own life. In God's mercy, He has given man a free will, but He wants that man choose life, choose Him. Psalm 115:15–16 says, "Ye are blessed of the LORD who made heaven and earth. The heaven, even the heavens, are the LORD's: but the earth hath he given to the children of men." He not only gave us a free will but decided to give us the earth to have dominion over it; you can read this in Genesis 1.

"And he said, I am Abraham's servant. And the LORD hath blessed my master greatly; and he is become great: and he hath given him flocks, and herds, and silver, and gold, and menservants, and maidservants, and camels, and asses."

Genesis 24:34–35

Abram's name originally meant "Exalted Father." Later God changed it to Abraham, which means "Father of a multitude." Why was he so blessed? Genesis 15:6 says that Abram believed God, and it was counted to him for righteousness. He trusted God and took Him at his word. God told him that he would be the father of many nations. Abram was an old man, and his wife was barren, but he believed God. He obeyed God. Obedience and trust bring blessings. God loves when we trust Him. Isaiah 1:19 states: "If ye be willing and obedient, ye shall eat the good of the land." As we trust God and believe that He is who He says He is, we will be blessed in every area of our life. Blessings will overtake us, and favor will be upon us and our children and our children's children. It will happen!

"So the LORD blessed the latter end of Job more than his beginning: for he had fourteen thousand sheep, and six thousand camels, and a thousand yoke of oxen, and a thousand she asses. He had also seven sons and three daughters."

Job 42:12–13

God is a God of restoration. It is Satan who steals and destroys, according to John 10:10. It is God who builds and replenishes, who gives life, also according to John 10:10. If you read the book of Job carefully, you will see that it was Satan who came in and stole and destroyed all that Job had. And in the very end, it was God who came in and blessed all that was stolen. He restored more than Job had in the beginning. Joel 2:25 speaks of how God restores all the years that the locust has eaten. Isaiah 61:7 reminds us that he will restore a double portion. If you have experienced your life being ripped from you, it would do you well to take these scriptures and hold on tight to them. Dare to believe them and see them come to pass in your life till every last thing that was stolen is replaced. Jesus has paid for this to happen.

"But his delight is in the law of the LORD; and in his law doth he meditate day and night. And he shall be like a tree planted by the rivers of water, that bringeth forth his fruit in his season; his leaf also shall not wither; and whatsoever he doeth shall prosper."

Psalm 1:2–3

His Word was meant to be delighted in. His Word can give us joy, and we can actually come to the point where we can fall in love with his Word, for it is alive.

John 1:14 says, "And the Word was made flesh, and dwelt among us, (and we beheld his glory, the glory as of the only begotten of the Father,) full of grace and truth." I have experienced loving the Word of God. I didn't used to, to be honest. I made the decision to think on and meditate on the Scriptures. I made myself refuse to think on my problems. Everyone has problems, but I decided to fix my mind on His Word throughout the day. It took a few months to get in the habit, but it began to change me from the inside out. It brought peace to my soul. It began to speak to me; I began to understand it. The Holy Spirit helped me and taught me in this. I became more grateful and less negative. But each day I had to choose this way. Things began to change for the better in every area of my life. Favor and blessings followed me.

"The LORD is my shepherd, I shall not want."

Psalm 23:1

If you have a shepherd, this means that you are a follower. It means someone else is sitting in the driver's seat. It also means He will provide for you. You will not be in any need or have any lack for anything. For what does a shepherd do? He protects and feeds. He provides for his sheep. He leads them out of harm's way. All the sheep does is feed and rest and enjoy the benefits of the shepherd. God loves to provide for His sheep, and He can do a much better job than you or I can. We can lead, but our lives will be greatly limited. If He leads, our life's potential will be unlimited.

So the end result will be: I shall not want for anything, physically or spiritually.

"O taste and see that the LORD is good: blessed is the man that trusteth in him. O fear the LORD, ye his saints: for there is no want to them that fear him. The young lions do lack and suffer hunger: but they that seek the LORD shall not want any good thing."

Psalm 34:8–10

Those who trust Him will also love His Word. You will trust His word and take Him at His word. His word is sweeter than honey; Psalm 119:103 says, "How sweet are thy words unto my taste! yea, sweeter than honey to my mouth!"

To fear the Lord is to revere Him. The lion may be hungry, may lack, but we who seek God, who revere Him and trust Him, will not lack any good thing. We will not need anything; He will take care of us and provide for us. We are blessed.

"I have been young, and now am old; yet have I not seen the righteous forsaken, nor his seed begging bread. He is ever merciful, and lendeth; and his seed is blessed."

Psalm 37:25–26

These are the words of King David. He is speaking of his whole life, from youth to being elderly. Throughout his life, he never saw the righteous forsaken, meaning they were never left. David lived a long life, and God always met their needs. God blessed him so that he was on the other end of the beggar. He was the lender, and his seed, or his children, were blessed. They probably saw the example of their parents and became lenders and blessed as well. Children learn what they live. David had a heart after God and so did his son Solomon.

"For with thee is the fountain of life:"

Psalm 36:9

We were made to be dependent creatures. As humans, we were made to drink and get thirsty on a regular basis. If we don't drink, we die. What makes us think it is any different spiritually? He is the fountain of life. The problem is that most people don't know there is such a fountain. We think we can make it on our own—we are the source of our lives. Our Father wants to be the source of our life. Within Him is the fountain. Only He can truly fill us and satisfy our longing hearts. Imagine being fully loved, blessed, and satisfied every single day. I believe it is possible, even on this earth. As we practice His presence and learn to come to Him to receive of His fullness through His word and His spirit, we shall walk in the blessing we were intended to walk in. Verse 8 states, "They shall be abundantly satisfied with the fatness of thy house; and thou shalt make them drink of the river of thy pleasures.

"Blessed is the man that maketh the LORD his trust."

Psalm 40:4

He is a smart man that trusts God. And reading this verse tells us we have to do it. We have to make the LORD our trust. When we do this, we are blessed because he will prove that His word can provide. Blessings will be the result of trusting.

"Blessed is he that considereth the poor: the LORD will deliver him in time of trouble. The LORD will preserve him and keep him alive; and he shall be blessed upon the earth: and thou wilt not deliver him unto the will of his enemies."

To consider is to think about, to understand, and to care about what the Lord cares about. When we take care of what is dear to Him, He will take care of what is dear to us. Luke 6:38 says, "Give, and it shall be given unto you; good measure, pressed down, and shaken together, shall men give into your bosom." But who is the one who puts it on men's hearts to give? If you deliver someone out of trouble, God will deliver you. Those who are blessed on the earth are the ones who are blessing others. They can't help it; it comes from the overflow of the good Father.

"Blessed be the LORD, who daily loadeth us with benefits, even the God of our salvation."

This word "loadeth" in Hebrew actually means to impose a burden on. He wants to bless you; His will is to load you with benefits and blessings. We should bless Him and thank Him, not whine and complain. In Psalm 23, it speaks of how "he anoints my head with oil, my cup runneth over." The Father is not thinking about the waste that spills over. He cares more that you realize. He cares more that you get to the point where you know that abundance belongs to you. God will never run out of blessings—that is impossible. He is the God of your salvation. He has saved you from death and poverty.

"Blessed are they that dwell in thy house: they will still be praising thee. Selah. Blessed is the man whose strength is in thee; in whose heart are the ways of them. Who passing through the valley of Baca make it a well; the rain also filleth the pools. They go from strength to strength, every one of them in Zion appeareth before God."

Psalm 84:4–7

Those who are keeping themselves God centered and Jesus centered by abiding in Him—those who live by His word, putting it first above circumstances and feelings—will find their strength in Him. They that love to worship and be in His presence and who keep fellowship with him—who are at home in His presence and in His word—will find their strength in Him and nowhere else. As they are connected with Him, He infuses His love, power, and ability to and through them.

Baca is the Hebrew word for weeping or mourning, even complaining. But as I read it and see that the people have their strength in the Lord, they only pass by it. They do not stay. They even make it a well. To have His strength is to wait on Him; to be still and be refreshed so that you are full. Strength to strength, glory to glory. We will not be complainers, for we do not need to be!

"For the LORD God is a sun and shield: the LORD will give grace and glory: no good thing will he withhold from them that walk uprightly."

Psalm 84:11

The earthly sun is blindingly bright, giving warmth and light to all who come in contact with it. It was created by God, the one whom light stems from. He is the source of all light and power and energy. He is our shield. The ones that walk uprightly will be the ones that benefit from Him the most; the ones who know Him. We are now in the new Covenant through the cross of Jesus. Through Jesus, grace and glory have been given freely. Jesus has provided all by His obedience, and He will withhold no good thing from his children; but we must receive it by faith through grace.

"The righteous shall flourish like the palm tree: he shall grow like a cedar in Lebanon. Those that be planted in the house of the LORD shall flourish in the courts of our God. They shall still bring forth fruit in old age; they shall be fat and flourishing; to shew that the LORD is upright: he is my rock, and there is no unrighteousness in him."

Psalm 92:12–14

The righteous run on different energy than the rest of the world. We have food that they do not know of and have never tasted. We just keep flourishing because of the Spirit and His Word and His presence. When a sponge is dry, it has to wait until it is soaked and wet to be full again. It is possible to never run dry but to have His rivers of living water flowing constantly, refreshing ourselves and everyone we come into contact with. We are the righteous in Christ Jesus. The cedars in Lebanon are tall, and you will see that some spread out horizontally. Plant yourself in the presence of the Lord often. When we worship, we get back into balance in our emotions. We get centered, receiving His precious peace. It doesn't matter how old we are or where we are in our walk, we can have fruit and an abundant life that is flourishing so that people can see it on our faces. This is a representation of the Lord—you are showing that He is upright.

"Blessed is the man whom thou chasteneth, O LORD, and teachest him out of thy law; that thou mayest give him rest from the days of adversity…"

Psalm 94:12–13

When you know that your Father loves you for who you are, you can handle his correction. He loves you so much that he is watching out for and thinking of your future, just like a good father here on the earth, who raises his son right and shows him the way to success. He cares about his son's future. He doesn't want to see him fail or sweating the rest of his life. A good father desires to see his child blessed, happy, healthy, and leading a very productive life.

"Who redeemeth thy life from destruction; who crowneth thee with lovingkindness and tender mercies; who satisfieth thy mouth with good things; so that thy youth is renewed like the eagle's."

Psalm 103:4–5

God is the one who redeems your life from destruction. He is the one who crowns you with lovingkindness and tender mercies. He satisfies your mouth with good things so that your youth is renewed like the eagle's. If you think about it, this is exactly what Jesus did on the cross for you. He provided a way for blessing, an avenue for wholeness. The good things in your mouth can be physical and spiritual. He created good food that is good for our bodies, but He also gave us his Word, as it says in Proverbs 4:20–23. It is the Scriptures that bring life to all that find them and healing to all of their flesh.

"Praise ye the LORD. Blessed is the man that feareth the LORD, that delighteth greatly in his commandments. His seed shall be mighty upon the earth: the generation of the upright shall be blessed. Wealth and riches shall be in his house: and his righteousness endureth forever."

Psalm 112:1–3

Blessed is the man that doesn't merely delight in His commandments but who also greatly delights in them. Be honest with yourself and think about what you take great delight in. Consider what that is and how it makes you feel. He wants us to feel that way about His Word.

For the seed to be mighty on the earth means that the parent has already been mighty first; the child follows suit. His generation will be blessed. Wealth and riches will be in the house of the righteous, and he will leave a legacy. His righteousness will endure forever; not because of us but because it is the righteousness of Jesus. It never ends but goes on forever.

"For every beast of the forest is mine, and the cattle upon a thousand hills."

Psalm 50:10

He who creates something is the owner of it, and he can do what he wants with his creation. God chooses to exercise His loving kindness on his creation. Imagine every beast of the world—hippos, bears, eagles, tigers, owls. Think of all the many kinds of species of animals. He has such an imagination. They are all His, and He created all of the different habitats they live in. Each type of food for them is also unique. He made them and everything they need to sustain them. He didn't miss a thing. To say the cattle upon a thousand hills are His is to say all animals are His.

"He will bless them that fear the LORD, both small and great. The LORD shall increase you more and more, you and your children. Ye are blessed of the LORD which made heaven and earth. The heaven, even the heavens, are the LORD's: but the earth hath he given to the children of men."

Psalm 115:13–16

The proud do not fear the Lord, for they do not need Him. They think they only need themselves; they are not humble. But those that are humble fear the Lord, and for this, they are blessed. You can be great and still be humble and fear the Lord. Look at David, for example. He was great, but he feared the Lord. What will happen to you when you do this is what happened to David. He will increase you more and more and your children as well. Can you picture yourself being blessed by the creator who made heaven and earth?

And that's not all. The heavens are His, but He even went so far as to give the earth to the children of men. This goes along with Genesis 1, in which He said He gave man dominion over the earth.

"O give thanks unto the LORD; for he is good: because his mercy endureth forever."

Psalm 119:1

We should give God thanks for all He has done and for His goodness. Too often we are focused on the problems of this world. And when the new day comes, well, we are so used to thinking on problems that if we don't have any, we will create new ones. It becomes, in a twisted way, a comfort zone. God's peace should be our only comfort zone.

"Blessed is every one that feareth the LORD; that walketh in his ways. For thou shall eat the labor of thy hands: happy shalt thou be, and it shall be well with thee."

Psalm 128:1–2

Again we see another scripture about fearing the Lord. These are the blessed ones, the ones who fear Him. When one fears the Lord, he is humbling himself and surrendering to God as higher than all—wiser and all powerful. When you are in total charge of your own life, you will not look to God or anyone else for guidance. When you look to Him, you are much better off, for He is the wisest of all and can see ahead, where we cannot. You will walk in His ways because you trust in Him. As you submit to Him, He will give you wisdom so that you can do good labor and then eat the fruit of that labor. And happy shall you be, and all shall be well with you.

"For he hath strengthened the bars of thy gates; he hath blessed thy children within thee. He maketh peace in thy borders, and filleth thee with the finest of the wheat. He sendeth forth his commandment upon the earth: his word runneth very swiftly."

Psalm 147:13–15

He has strengthened the bars of your gates because he is your defender, your protector. All that you have is blessed; rest upon this truth. Your children in the womb are blessed, and so expect them to be formed by His hands as whole and healthy. He is your provider, not just filling your house with wheat, but the finest of wheat. His word is alive and powerful, sharp and quick. He sent His word, which is Jesus; Jesus and the Word are one. As He sends forth His word, it does not return void or empty. It is truth, and it does what it has set out to do. His word runs very swiftly; trust it.

"Now therefore hearken unto me, O ye children: for blessed are they that keep my ways. Hear instruction, and be wise, refuse it not. Blessed is the man that heareth me, watching daily at my gates, waiting at the posts of my doors. For whoso findeth me findeth life, and shall obtain favour of the LORD."

Proverbs 8:32–35

It is a good thing to remain humble and teachable. Avoid pride, for it will prevent your ability to be taught and to learn from him. His word will make you wise, so do not refuse it.

Listen and watch daily for His wisdom. Be slow to speak and swift to listen. Wait and be patient, not anxious and hasty. When a person finds it, that means he has been looking. And as you seek it, you will find life. And at the same time you will get favor from the Lord. He is so pleased when His children trust Him.

"He becometh poor that dealeth with a slack hand: but the hand of the diligent maketh rich. He that gathereth in summer is a wise son: but he that sleepeth in harvest is a son that causeth shame. Blessings are upon the head of the just: but violence covereth the mouth of the wicked. The memory of the just is blessed…"

Proverbs 10:4–7

To be slack means to be lazy. So if you are slow and lazy in giving, you will become poor. This makes no sense to most people, but when you understand the kingdom's ways, you will know that to give is to plant seeds, which means that they will multiply and give you a harvest. Be diligent to plant seed; doing it with a right and joyful heart will increase you. It will make you rich. God will bless the work of your hands. Can you imagine sleeping in the middle of a harvest? Here you plant a garden, water it, and tend for the weeds and when the time comes to harvest, you close your door and just go to sleep. Blessings are on your head if you are His child.

All that is about you is blessed, even the memory of you, even your words and the end result of what your words produce. Not so with the evil. You know a tree by its fruit, and out of the evil come bad words and bad fruit. Even the memory of them gives a sad and regretful taste to the one who remembers them. You can choose to be a drain on people or a fountain that will bless. It is your choice.

"He that hath a bountiful eye shall be blessed; for he giveth of his bread to the poor."

Proverbs 22:9

Again, here is an example of a giver, a bountiful sower. Even his thoughts are not stingy and skimpy. Even his eye sees things through a giver's eye. He is always thinking, "What can I do for them? How can I help?" He considers the poor. He doesn't ignore and pass them. He stops to look at them. How many times do we pull up to a stop light, where there is a homeless person, and we turn the other way and pretend they will go away. We try to make them disappear. Yes, we have to use wisdom, but in doing so, we don't have to ignore them. The one with the bountiful eye gives bread to the poor.

"She openeth her mouth with wisdom; and in her tongue is the law of kindness. She looketh well to the ways of her household, and eateth not the bread of idleness. Her children arise up, and call her blessed; her husband also, and he praiseth her."

Proverbs 31:26–28

Let us look deeper. Out of the abundance of the heart the mouth speaks. This truly stems from the thoughts she thinks and dwells on. Remember, as a man thinks in his heart, so is he. She, therefore, thought and saw kindness, wisdom, and blessing her family; she thought of being busy, to do well for them.

We can choose to be what we want. We can be a victim, and if we do, we'll think like a victim and picture ourselves that way. We'll think that everyone is out to get us. You will attract what you think, but you can change that and think on the good instead. See yourself as a blessing, and speak blessings over yourself. Think something like, "I am a blessing to my family. I lean on the strength and wisdom of the Lord to help me every day. I follow His lead and not my own." Your children will bless and praise you, not curse you. Your husband will praise you in the gates. He will trust you because you give him reason to trust you.

"Then shall he give the rain of thy seed, that thou shalt sow the ground withal; and bread of increase of the earth, and it shall be fat and plenteous: in that day shall thy cattle feed in large pastures."

Isaiah 30:23

He is our God and our source for all things. He gives us seed, and He gives us rain to water the seed. His way is not only to supply our needs but to supply with an abundant supply. An earthly father would give a good inheritance to His children but may always hope for more to leave—the more the better. God is so capable of supplying richly and continually with love. The real problem lies in us not receiving or believing. We don't think He wants to do these things for us. Notice the very last phrase: in large pastures. That is our Father in heaven. According to your faith, be it done unto you, my friend.

"But the liberal deviseth liberal things; and by liberal things shall he stand."

Isaiah 32:8

From The Message:

"But generous people plan to do what is generous. And they stand firm in their generosity."

To devise is to plan. There are some who enjoy devising evil and trickery. There are others who devise with thoughts of greed and consuming goods. They think on the next thing that they want to buy or collect. How different is it to think on and plan and devise ways of giving, as well as people to bless, and to imagine and create projects that will benefit others in your city, in your church, in your state, in your country, or in other countries around the world. His Spirit and that same generous spirit live in you if you know Jesus.

"And my people shall dwell in a peaceable habitation, and in sure dwellings, and in quiet resting places;"

Isaiah 32:18

Speak this one over your household and over your family. With Christ living in you, you have peace with God. You have peace living inside of you. This is a peace from heaven, one that passes all understanding. In your circumstances, there may be turmoil even all around, but it is possible for you, even through the turmoil, to be at peace and to not be moved. In the world you will have tribulation, but be of good cheer, Jesus said, "I have overcome the world." He will keep you and sustain you in the eye of the storm.

"Look unto Abraham your father, and unto Sarah that bare you: for I called him alone, and blessed him, and increased him."

Isaiah 51:2

God is speaking to those who follow after righteousness. You can read the verse that comes before and see it for yourself. He says to look at Abraham, to think on his life. Remember how God blessed him. You can read about him in Genesis 12. God told him that He would make of him a great nation, that He would make his name great, and that he would be a blessing. God said He would bless them that bless him and curse them that curse him. This blessing all came from God the good father. God is the one who increased him for that, remember, is God's way.

"Blessed is the man that trusteth in the LORD, and whose hope the LORD is. For he shall be as a tree planted by the waters, and that spreadeth out her roots by the river, and shall not see when heat cometh, but her leaf shall be green; and shall not be careful in the year of drought, neither shall cease from yielding fruit."

Jeremiah 17:7–8

My help in is the Lord, not in man. My hope is in the Lord and not in anything or anyone else. I shall be blessed because I trust in Him. I am as a tree planted by the waters, very strong and secure. By trusting in Him, I will be sustained. It is by my trust in His word that I will grow and my leaf shall always be green.

I will not see when heat comes, because I won't be looking for it. I shall be keeping my eyes on the Lord. I will not be leading my life according to circumstances nor letting feelings guide my every step. It is possible to always be the same calm and peaceful person, never worried about the unpredictable weather or any threatening drought. It is possible to live with a continual harvest of fruit. Do not follow the world's way. It is by following God's kingdom principles that this is all possible.

"Bring ye all the tithes into the storehouse, that there may be meat in mine house, and prove me now herewith, saith the LORD of hosts, if I will not open you the windows of heaven, and pour you out a blessing, that there shall not be room enough to receive it. And I will rebuke the devourer for your sakes, and he shall not destroy the fruits of your ground; neither shall your vine cast her fruit before the time in the field, saith the LORD of hosts. And all nations shall call you blessed: for you shall be a delightsome land, saith the LORD of hosts."

Malachi 3:10-12

The word "all" does not mean that God is demanding every cent we have in a selfish way; His heart is to give and hold nothing back. He gives all of His blessing. He wants us to have the same heart—a giving attitude. You cannot out give God. Picture the windows of heaven opening out onto you, pouring out more than you need. Not only does He bless you back, but He rebukes the devourer for your sake. The devourer will not destroy the fruit of your ground, and your harvest will come right on time. You will be so blessed that all the nations will see it, and they shall call you blessed. The Lord of hosts is the one who has spoken all of this. If He declares it, it shall be so. Lastly, He states that you shall be a delightsome land! You are truly blessed. To give to the Lord is more for your good than anything else.

(Speaking of Abraham) "That in blessing I will bless thee, and in multiplying I will multiply thy seed as the stars of the heaven, and as the sand which is upon the sea shore; and thy seed shall possess the gate of his enemies; And in thy seed shall all the nations of the earth be blessed; because thou hast obeyed my voice."

Genesis 22:17–18

Our Father God gives a parallel using the stars and the grains of sand to explain just how much He will bless and multiply the seed of Abraham. Can you count the stars? Can anyone count the sand? The next phrase, I believe, is prophetic, speaking of Jesus and His finished work, the defeat of the enemy. He is the one who holds the keys of death and hell. "Thy seed shall possess the gate of his enemies." It is because of Jesus that we are blessed and included in Abraham's blessing. Galatians 3:29: "And if ye be Christ's, then are ye Abraham's seed, and heirs according to the promise."

"Then Isaac sowed in that land, and received in the same year an hundredfold: and the LORD blessed him. And the man waxed great, and went forward, and grew until he became very great: For he had possession of flocks, and possession of herds, and great store of servants: and the Philistines envied him."

Genesis 26:12–14

This is a perfect picture of how I believe a child of God could and should be living; it displays God's best. And he waxed great; he went forward, not backward. He grew and kept growing until he became very great. We are to prosper so much that we can't help but be the envy of the world around us. We should be the ones to loan and not borrow. The very first words in this passage are "Then Isaac sowed in that land." We are meant to be sowers and reapers, givers and blessers.

"And it shall come to pass, if thou shalt hearken diligently unto the voice of the LORD thy God, to observe and to do all his commandments which I command thee this day, that the LORD thy God will set thee on high above all nations of the earth: And all these blessings shall come on thee, and overtake thee, if thou shalt hearken unto the voice of the LORD thy God. Blessed shalt thou be in the city, and blessed shalt thou be in the field. Blessed shall be the fruit of thy body, and the fruit of thy ground, and the fruit of thy cattle, the increase of thy kine, and the flocks of thy sheep. Blessed shall be thy basket and thy store. Blessed shalt thou be when thou comest in, and blessed shalt thou be when thou goest out. The LORD shall cause thine enemies that rise up against thee to be smitten before thy face: they shall come out against thee one way, and flee before thee seven ways. The LORD shall command the blessing upon thee in thy storehouses, and in all that thou settest thine hand unto; and he shall bless thee in the land which the LORD thy God giveth thee."

Deuteronomy 28:1–8

In the Old Testament, in order to receive the blessings of God, you needed to be willing and obedient. In the New Testament, we receive these blessings by faith in Christ Jesus (Gal. 3:13–14). Verse 29 of this same chapter says, "And if ye be Christ's, then are ye Abraham's seed, and heirs according to the promise." Jesus did all the work on the cross and provided all that we would ever need. Healing is a gift. Provision is a gift. Peace with God is a gift. The blessings of God are gifts; we cannot buy them or earn them. They are free from God through Jesus because He loves us greatly. Receive these blessings. You are blessed in every area of your life, from your property, to your animals and gardens, to your family and your bank accounts. Speak these blessings over yourself often and see them operating in your life. See the enemy fleeing seven ways away from you. The favor of God is all around you, so what or whom shall we fear? We belong on the winning side.

"I call heaven and earth to record this day against you, that I have set before you life and death, blessing and cursing: therefore choose life, that both thou and thy seed may live:"

Deuteronomy 30:19

God asks us to choose. We are the ones who have the freedom to choose; He cannot make us. He gave us a free will. No one is twisting your arm. No one can make you happy but you. God has already given His Son, and Jesus has already defeated Satan.

John 10:10 says, "I am come that they might have life, and that they might have it more abundantly." Not everyone is going to experience this abundant life. We are going to have to make a decision to take it for ourselves. He went through so much for you and me. He has given us everything. Choose to respond to that love by accepting the gift He gave us.

"He becometh poor that dealeth with a slack hand: but the hand of the diligent maketh rich. He that gathereth in summer is a wise son: but he that sleepeth in harvest is a son that causeth shame. Blessings are upon the head of the just: but violence covers the mouth of the wicked. The memory of the just is blessed:"

Proverbs 10:4–7

There is so much here. You can take one phrase at a time and just think on it. You can have a slack hand in giving, which means you have a lazy hand; you are slow to give. You will become poor this way. The hand of the diligent will make them rich because they keep planting, keep giving, and keep obeying God's voice. To gather in the summer is wise. To be ready when the harvest time comes is wise. Don't be lazy; don't be slack—be ready. It will pay off. Blessings are on the head of the just, and they come from God, the maker of heaven and earth. Even the memory of the righteous is blessed.

"The labour of the righteous tendeth to life: the fruit of the wicked to sin."

Proverbs 10:16

Their labor tends to life because they are a blessed people. The righteous trust in their God. He is their Jehovah, their good Shepherd. Everything that they touch is blessed. They live in obedience to Him. Their heart is to serve and to bless. Their words are spoken in wisdom to bring life, so it makes sense that their labor tends only to life. Romans 8:5–6 says, "For they that are after the flesh do mind the things of the flesh; but they that are after the Spirit the things of the Spirit. For to be carnally minded is death; but to be spiritually minded is life and peace."

"The blessing of the LORD, it maketh rich, and he addeth no sorrow with it."

Proverbs 10:22

We can try to force circumstances to happen. We can struggle in our own strength, but when we trust the Lord's provision and patiently wait for His timing, we will experience His blessing in our lives. When He provides, the blessing is rich, and when we do it, we are so limited. There is no sorrow that comes with the Lord's blessing, only joy—unspeakable joy. It is He who makes us rich.

"By the blessing of the upright the city is exalted: but it is overthrown by the mouth of the wicked."

Proverbs 11:11

Wherever the blessed man is, everything around him will be blessed. If he works in a particular job, that business will see blessing and growth. His children will be blessed. Read through Deuteronomy 28 and discover the blessings we are to be walking in. Out of the upright come blessings. He should be speaking with the wisdom and mercy of God, representing God to others. Yes, even the city will be blessed because he is there; for he will be blessing his city and praying for his city. Not so with the wicked.

"There is that scattereth, and yet increaseth; and there is that withholdeth more than is meet, but it tendeth to poverty. The liberal soul shall be made fat: and he that watereth shall be watered also himself."

Proverbs 11:24–25

If we think of a garden again, we can get a clearer picture of this scripture. A farmer would not expect any garden to grow by wishing for it. He knows he must plant seed, and he realizes he must plant the seed of the vegetable that he wishes to harvest. This is exactly how the Kingdom of God operates; you give and plant in good soil, and you are sowing into eternity. God is the one who brings the increase and multiplies the seed sown. If you withhold, you will see no multiplication. It's an attitude of generosity that will cause blessing in all areas of your life. A stingy man is a man full of stress and fear.

"He that trusteth in his riches shall fall: but the righteous shall flourish as a branch."

It is the love of money that is the root of all evil. We were meant and made to trust our creator, God our Father. He loves when we trust Him. We were not made or meant to trust in anything created, whether it be a person, animal, or a thing. They are only a creation just like us. They cannot come through for us, for they are temporary on this earth, just as we are. If we trust in God, we will be blessed. He will cause us to grow, to bloom as a lush and fruitful branch. All will see and praise our God!

"The fruit of the righteous is a tree of life; and he that winneth souls is wise. Behold, the righteous shall be recompensed in the earth…"

Proverbs 11:30–31

Many scriptures speak of our words, the fruit of our lips. The righteous speak words of life, planting good seed with their words. They speak the word of God, which is good seed, full of power and life. That seed grows as we speak it. It grows in the hearts of men, bringing them to the Lord. As we do this, we are wise. Rather than wasting our words we cause them to work for the good of the kingdom. We shall be recompensed in the earth, meaning we shall be rewarded and be in peace.

"The slothful man roasteth not that which he took in hunting: but the substance of a diligent man is precious."

Proverbs 12:27

Why would you not roast what you hunted? Because it was too much work? This means that you wouldn't eat. God gave us two arms and two legs. He gave us strength for a reason, as well as a mind to think. As we make a choice to use these things, we will reap the benefits of our labor. The substance of a diligent man is precious due to his diligence. Diligence means "Constant and earnest effort to accomplish what is undertaken; persistent exertion of body or mind." Our work pays off.

"He that tilleth his land shall be satisfied with bread: but he that followeth vain persons is void of understanding."

Proverbs 12:11

Amplified

"He who tills his land shall be satisfied with bread, but he who follows worthless pursuits is lacking in sense and is without understanding."

The bottom line is God gave us strength for a reason. While we look to Him for His wisdom and are led by His Spirit, we still must be willing to work. It is God who will bless our work and our efforts. But if we don't work, we won't eat. He can't bless nothing. God's way is that we grow and increase. We should be the most blessed people on this earth.

"A man's belly shall be satisfied with the fruit of his mouth; and with the increase of his lips shall he be filled. Death and life are in the power of the tongue: and they that love it shall eat the fruit thereof."

Proverbs 18:20–21

Just as you are filled with physical food by inserting it into your mouth and into your stomach, your life will be satisfied by the fruit of words that come out of your mouth. You will have what you speak. The same is true with the increase of the physical food we eat as we eat more and more and are filled. As you speak with your words and increase those words more and more, your life will show what you speak. You have power in your tongue for either life or death. It is your choice. If you speak death, that is what you shall have. If you speak life, life is what you shall have. Now, when you love a particular fruit, you will probably be buying and eating that kind of fruit often. The more you give your tongue to speaking life, the sooner it may come. As you give yourself to His word, to meditate on it day and night, so shall you have good success. You are loving that fruit, those good words that you are speaking will bring to life exactly what you speak. There is power in your tongue.

"He that hath pity upon the poor lendeth unto the LORD; and that which he hath given will he pay him again."

Proverbs 19:17

Amplified

"He who has pity on the poor lends to the LORD, and that which he has given He will repay to him."

When we give to the poor, it is from God's heart. It is His heart to bless them and to give to them. We are His hands. His compassion moves on us. So you can think of it as a loan; as you give to the poor, God will give back to you.

"The thoughts of the diligent tend only to plenteousness; but of every one that is hasty only to want."

Proverbs 21:5

This is because a diligent person does not procrastinate. Instead, they think ahead and anticipate. They don't even waste their thoughts. They know that time is precious, and much time can be wasted just by thinking on nothing, whether it be cares, anxieties, or any of the things of this world. The diligent plan, sow, and reap using kingdom principles and the wisdom of God. They seek God and His thoughts. The hasty never consult God. They look to their own wisdom. In the end, they always fall short.

"A faithful man shall abound with blessings…"

Proverbs 28:20

We read many scriptures regarding sowing and reaping. A righteous man who is faithful in sowing continually shall also reap continually. We know that seed multiplies, and so it is a law that as he sows with a cheerful heart into good soil, he shall have an abundance of harvest. It's only a matter of time. Give, and it shall be given.

"For I will pour water upon him that is thirsty, and floods upon the dry ground: I will pour my spirit upon thy seed, and my blessing upon thine offspring."

Isaiah 44:3

God is the one who waters, feeds, and blesses. Blessing originated from our God. He doesn't curse; He blesses. When our thirst is quenched, we should thank God. When our dry ground is watered and nourished, we give thanks where thanks is due—our Creator. He pours his Spirit on our seed, which is our children. He is the one who blesses our offspring. It is a natural progression, and we should anticipate it, welcoming His blessing and always thanking Him for it.

About the Author

Linda Patarello is a born again Christian, and graduate from Charis Bible College in Colorado Springs, Colorado. She currently lives there, and spends most of her time spreading the truth about God's Love from the written Word. Linda is a California native with broad experience in leading praise & worship and songwriting. She believes that the highest calling is to worship the "Giver of All Gifts." She also believes we are born to pursue a relationship with God the Father, Jesus Christ and the Holy Spirit, and to share it with others. Her vision is to help people find true love for the Word of God, and to uncover its precious truths that are waiting to be revealed.

For More Information or to Contact the Author, Please Write to:

Linda Patarello
P.O. Box 7964
Colorado Springs, CO 80933

www.Heartsower.com

Prayer of Salvation

There is nothing more fulfilling in life than knowing that God loves you. God has made, and continues to make His love known to us by having sent His only begotten son, Jesus Christ, to die on the cross as payment for our sins and the injustices done unto us.

Has anyone willingly given up their life in exchange for yours, so that you may live? Jesus did. "Greater love hath no man than this, that a man lay down his life for his friends" (Jn. 15:13). Notice, that Jesus said this *before* he went to the cross. He laid down His life for us because he saw you and I, his friends, benefiting from this act of love.

You were the joy that was set before Jesus. "For the joy that was set before him [he] endured the cross, despising the shame, and is set down at the right hand of the throne of God" (Heb. 12:2). Only a true, selfless friend could love like this. Would you like to know the One Who finds you valuable, Who truly loves you? If you would like to ask Jesus to be your friend and your Lord and Savior, you can ask Him today. You can use your own words or pray,

"Lord Jesus, I want to know you, I want to be your friend. I invite you into my life, so that I may know you more. Be my saving friend, Lord and Savior. I am sorry for all my sins and past mistakes. Thank you for forgiving me and loving me, in spite of my past. You are my friend, even when I have no one else. I want to receive everything you have for me, even your Holy Spirit. Take control of my life, and through my relationship with you, let it grow and mature, and become a light unto others. Thank you for freeing me from sin and darkness, and for putting me in right-standing with you forever. I am saved! Thank you, Jesus! Amen!

If you prayed this prayer for the first time in your life, we believe that you are born again! Find a good Bible-based church, and connect with other believers. Please share your testimony or visit us online:

http://www.orionproductions.tv/contact-us.html

You can write to us:

Orion Productions

PO Box 51194
Colorado Springs, CO 80949

Blessings to you! From our staff at Orion Productions.

To make known the stories and accounts
of God's work in people's lives
through multimedia products and
services.

Our latest publishing information can be found
by visiting our website at:

www.orionproductions.tv/publishing.html

www.ingramcontent.com/pod-product-compliance
Lightning Source LLC
Chambersburg PA
CBHW060635030426
42337CB00018B/3376